Doctor Knickerbocker
and Other Rhymes

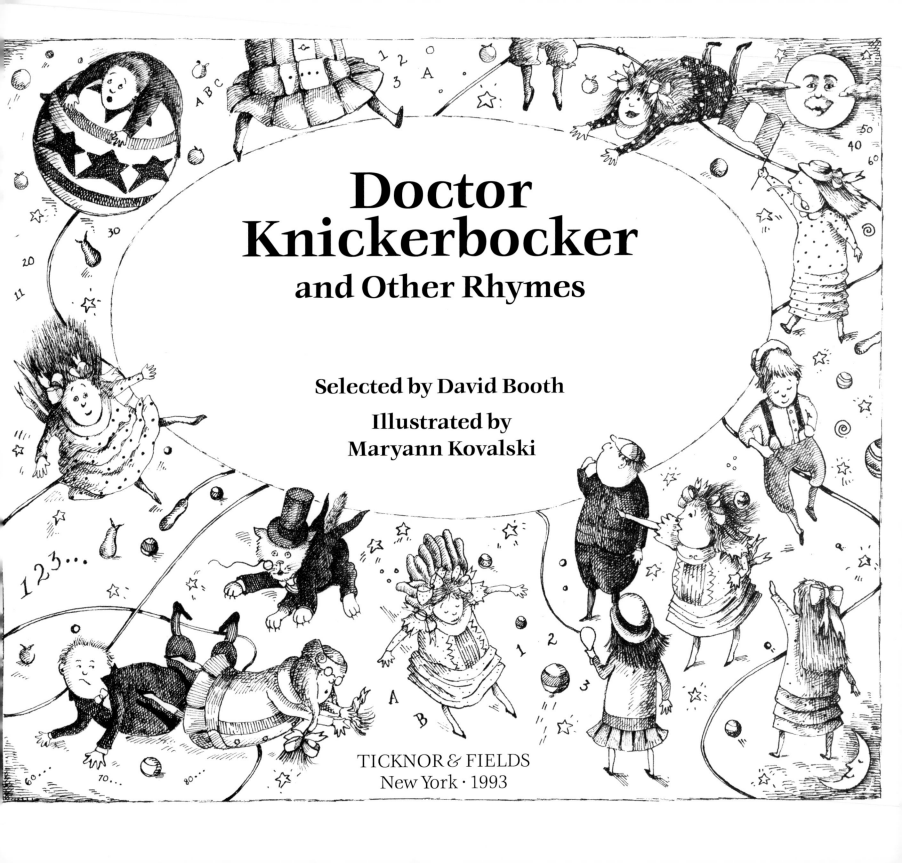

Doctor Knickerbocker
and Other Rhymes

Selected by David Booth

Illustrated by
Maryann Kovalski

TICKNOR & FIELDS
New York · 1993

First American edition 1993 published by Ticknor & Fields, A Houghton Mifflin Company,
215 Park Avenue South, New York, New York 10003.

First published in Canada by Kids Can Press Ltd.

Library of Congress Cataloging-in-Publication Data

Booth, David.
Doctor Knickerbocker and other rhymes / selected by David Booth;
illustrated by Maryann Kovalski—1st American ed.
p. cm.
Includes index.
Summary: A selection of poetry, much of it humorous, which
includes tongue twisters, jump rope rhymes, counting-out rhymes,
ball bounces, and autograph verse.
ISBN 0-395-67168-X
1. Children's poetry, Canadian. [1. Canadian poetry—Collections.
2. Humorous poetry.] I. Kovalski, Maryann, ill. II. Title.
PR9199.3.B595D6 1993
811' .54—dc20   92-46266   CIP   AC

Manufactured in Hong Kong.

10 9 8 7 6 5 4 3 2 1

For Michael Hermiston

D.B.

For Joanna

M.K.

I wish to thank Larry Swartz and his grade five students
at Queenston Drive Public School for their help in discovering
all the rhymes on their playground.
And Marion Seary, for reading the manuscript and offering
such helpful suggestions.

D.B.

Contents

Had a little sports car 298,
And I ran around a corner
And I slammed on the brakes.
 I bumped into a lady,
  I bumped into a man,
  I bumped into a policeman,
   Man oh man!

  Policeman caught me , put me in jail,
   All I had was ginger ale.
  How many bottles did I have?
   1, 2, 3, 4 ...

Out Loud, Right Now!

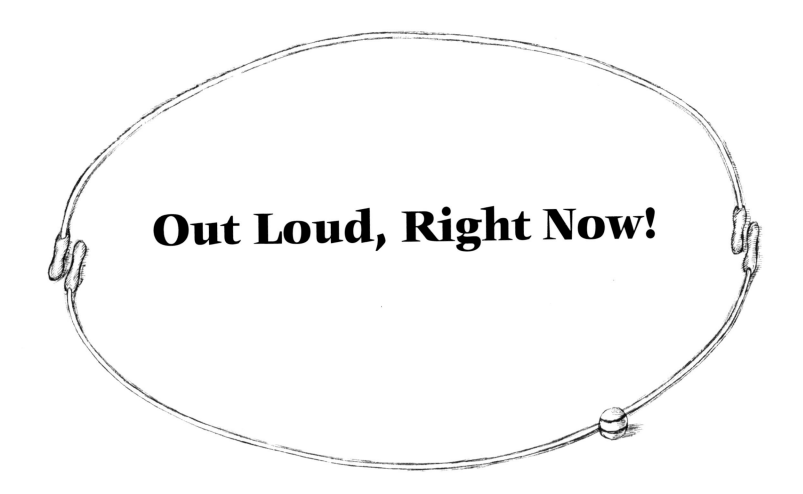

When I eat my Smarties, I eat the blue ones last. I suck them very

I'm a little acorn brown,
Lying on the cold, cold ground.
Everybody steps on me,
That's why I'm a nut,
you see.

I'm a nut, tuh, tuh,
I'm a nut, tuh, tuh,
I'm a nut in a rut, you see.

I call myself on the phone
Just to see if I'm at home.
I ask myself on a date,
The latest time is half-past eight.

I'm a nut, tuh, tuh,
I'm a nut, tuh, tuh,
I'm a nut in a rut, you see.

Pigs like mud,
Cows like squash!
I like you ~
I do, by gosh.

2

slowly, I crunch them very fast. I never eat the chocolate, I always eat the shell. When I eat my Smarties, I eat them very well.

Peter, Peter, if you're able,
Get your elbows off the table.
This is not a horse's stable,
But a ritzy dining table.

3

4

Doctor Knickerbocker, Knickerbocker, number nine,
I just got back and I'm feeling fine.

So let's hear the rhythm of the head, ding dong.

Now we got the rhythm of the head,
So let's hear the rhythm of the feet, stomp, stomp.

Now we got the rhythm of the feet,
So let's hear the rhythm of the hands, clap, clap.

Now we got the rhythm of the hands ...

Doctor Knickerbocker, Knickerbocker, number nine,
I just got back and I'm feeling fine.

Hot-cross buns, Hot-cross buns, One-a-penny, Two-a-penny, Hot-cross buns.

I woke up Sunday morning
And looked upon the wall.
The bedbugs and the beetles
Were having a game of ball.

The score was six to seven,
The beetles were ahead.
The beetles hit a home run,
And knocked me out of bed.

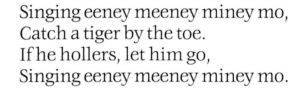

Singing eeney meeney miney mo,
Catch a tiger by the toe.
If he hollers, let him go,
Singing eeney meeney miney mo.

Who ate a bun? You are the one.

March, April, May,

June, July, August, September, October, November, December!

Billy gave me apples,
Billy gave me pears,
Billy gave me fifty cents
And kissed me on the stairs.

I gave him back his apples,
I gave him back his pears,
I gave him back his fifty cents
And kicked him down the stairs.

1, 2, 3, 4...

Hot potato,
pass it on,
pass it on, pass it on.
Who's got the hot potato?

And this is what she sent me for:

Salt... Vinegar... Pepper!

10

Old John Tucker was a mighty man,
He washed his face in a frying pan,
He combed his hair with a wagon wheel,
And had a toothache in his heel.
So get out of the way, old John Tucker,
You're too late to get your supper.

I'm a raindrop,
I'm a raindrop,
I'm a raindrop in the air.
But I'd rather be a raindrop
Than a drip from
over there.

Happy birthday to you,
You live in a zoo,
You look like
a monkey,
And you act like one,
too!

Happy birthday to you,
Smashed tomatoes
and stew,
Bread and butter
in the gutter,
Happy birthday
to you!

Charley went over the ocean,
Charley went over the sea.
Charley caught a codfish —
You can't catch me!

Over the lake,
Over the sea,
Over the ocean blue.

Up the river,
Down the river,
Out goes you!

Hickory, dickory,
Six and seven,
Abalonee, crack-a-bonee,
Ten and eleven,
Spin, spun, muskadit,
Ninety-nine, you are it!

Hey, Peter!
  I think I hear my name.
Hey, Peter!
  I think I hear it again.
You're wanted on the telephone!
  If it's not Greg, then I'm not home.

Hey, Greg!
  I think I hear my name.
Hey, Greg!
  I think I hear it again.
You're wanted on the telephone!
  If it's not Jim, then I'm not home.

Hey, Jim!
  I think I hear my name ...

Eeka locka
Horse's caca
Eeka locka
Out!

One, two, three, four,
Mary at the cottage door.
Five, six, seven, eight,
Eating cherries off a plate.
O - U - T spells out.

13

The wonder ball
Goes round and round.
Pass it quickly
Or you'll be bound.
If you're the one
To hold it last,
Then for you
This game is past.
YOU ARE OUT!

Miss Mary had a steamboat,

The [steamboat] had a [bell],

Ding, ding!

Miss Mary went to [heaven],

The steamboat went to ...

Hello operator,

Please give me number 9,

And if you disconnect me,

I'll [kick] your ...

Behind the yellow [curtain],

There was a piece of [glass].

Miss Mary [sat] upon it

And poked her little ...

Ask me no more ? ? ?,

Please tell me no more lies,

The [boys] are in the [bathroom]

Doing up their ...

The [flies] are in the [city],

The [bees] are in the [park],

Miss Mary and her boyfriend

Are [kiss]ing in the dark dark dark.

Teacher said, "That's not fair! Give me back my underwear."

I went into the house.
    Just like me.
I went upstairs.
    Just like me.
I went into a room.
    Just like me.
I looked in the glass.
    Just like me.
I saw a monkey.
    Just like me.

Mama Said It
and I Say It Too

Postman,
postman,
Do your duty.
Send this letter
To my cutie.
Don't you stop
Nor don't delay.
Get it to her
Right away.

If you think you
are in love,
And still there
is some question,
Don't worry much
about it,
It may be
indigestion.

CARTER'S
LITTLE
LIVER
PILLS
TRADE MARK

When you
fall in the river
There is a boat,
When you fall in the well
There is a rope,
When you fall in love
There is no
hope.

22

Vegetable Love,
Do you carrot all for me?
My heart beets for you.
With your turnip nose
And your radish face,
You are a peach.
If we cantaloupe,
Lettuce marry;
Weed make a swell pear.

When you see a monkey up a tree,
Pull on his tail and think of me.

Roses are red,
    Violets are blue,

What you need
    Is a good shampoo.

Through the teeth,
Past the gums,
Look out, stomach,
Here it comes!

Mind your own business
And don't mind mine.
Kiss your own sweetheart
And don't kiss mine.

I saw you in the ocean,
I saw you in the sea,
I saw you in the bathtub,
Oops! Pardon me!

When you get married
And your wife has twins,
Just call on me for safety pins.

Tarzan, Tarzan, in the air,
Tarzan lost his underwear.
Tarzan say, "Me no care.
Me no wear no underwear!"

Mary had a little lamb,
Its fleece was white as snow,
And everywhere that Mary went,
—She took it on a bus.

Mary had a little lamb,
Her father shot it dead.
And now it goes to school with her
Between two chunks of bread.

Mary had a little lamb,
It was a greedy glutton.
She fed it ice-cream all day long,
And now it's frozen mutton.

Mary had a little lamb,
You've heard this tale before,
But did you know she passed her plate
And had a little more?

Mary had a little cow,
It fed on safety pins.
And every time she milked the cow,
The milk came out in tins.

Way down south where bananas grow, A grasshopper stepped on an elephant's toe. The elephant said, with tears in his eyes, "Pick on someone more your own size."

28

The funniest thing I've ever seen
Was a tomcat sewing on a sewing machine.
Oh, the sewing machine got running too slow,
And it took seven stitches in the tomcat's toe.

Mother, may I take a swim?

Yes, my darling daughter,
But hang your clothes on a
hickory limb,
And don't go near the water.

What's the time?
Time you bought a watch!

The same time as it was this time yesterday.

What's the time?
About now.

What's the time?
Ten o'clock next Wednesday.

A minute to the next.

What's the time?
Time you knew better.

What's the time?

What's the time?

Half past, quarter to strike, ten minutes to the lamp-post.

What's

What's the time?
Half past kissing time and time to kiss again.

What's

Who stole the cookie from the cookie jar?

Nancy stole the cookie from the cookie jar.

Who, me?

Yes, you.

Couldn't be!

Then who?

Jenny stole the cookie from the cookie jar.

Who, me?

Yes, you.

Then who?

Couldn't be!

Charlie Chaplin
went to France
To teach the pretty girls
to dance.
First one heel,
Then the toe,
Do the splits
And around you go.
Salute to the captain,
Curtsey to the queen,
Touch the bottom
of the submarine.

On the mountain stands a school,
And in that school there is a desk,
And on that desk there is a book,
And in that book there is my name.
Ten boys' names must I know;
Wish me luck for here I go:
David, Billy, John,
Robert, Paul, Mark,
Peter, Gordon, Kenneth,
Joe.

Cinderelli, dressed
in yelli,
Went upstairs to
kiss a felli.
Made a mistake
And kissed a
snake.
How many doctors
did it take?
1, 2, 3, 4 ...

Motorboat, motorboat, go so slow,
Motorboat, motorboat, get up and go.
Motorboat, motorboat, go so fast,
Motorboat, motorboat, step on the gas!

33

Are you coming out, sir?
No, sir.
Why, sir?
Because I've got a cold, sir.
Where'd you get the cold, sir?
At the North Pole, sir.
What were you doing there, sir?
Catching polar bears, sir.
How many did you catch, sir?
One, sir, two, sir, three, sir,
That's enough for me, sir.

Eenie, meenie, minie, mo.
Catch a tiger by the toe;
If he hollers make him pay
Fifty dollars every day.
Out goes Y-O-U !

This is the way you spell Tennessee. One asee, two asee, three asee, four asee,

Monkey in the jailhouse,
Don't you hear him holler?
Took a pickle from a fish,
And didn't pay a dollar.
One, two, three,
Out goes she.

Fireman, fireman, number eight,
Hit his head against the gate.
The gate flew in, the gate flew out,
That's the way he put the fire out.
O-U-T spells out,
And out you go.

five asee, six asee, seven asee, eight asee, nine asee, Tennessee!

36

37

The elephant is a pretty bird,
It flits from bough to bough.
It builds its nest in a rhubarb tree,
And whistles like a cow.

Ladies and gentlemen, take my advice, pull down your pants and slide on the ice.

Nobody likes me, everybody hates me,
Guess I'll eat some worms.
Itsy-bitsy tiny ones,
Slippy, slurpy, grimy ones,
Look at those little things squirm.

First one was easy,
Second one was greasy,
Third one got stuck in my throat.
Hasten, Jason, call Dr. Mason,
Get these ghastly things out!

WELCOME MAMAS AND PAPAS
A fly and a flea flew up in a flue. Said the fly to the flea, "What shall we do?" "Let's fly," said the flea. "Let's flee," said the fly. So they flew up a flaw in the flue.
How much wood would a woodchuck chuck If a woodchuck could chuck wood? He would chuck what wood a woodchuck could chuck If a woodchuck could chuck wood.
If Peter Piper picked a peck of pickled peppers, A peck of pickled peppers Peter Piper picked. But if Peter Piper picked a peck of pickled peppers, Where is the peck of pickled peppers Peter Piper picked?

Popeye the sailor man, He lived in a caravan. He opened the door

And fell to the floor, Popeye the sailor man.

43

I'm Chiquita Banana, and I'm here to say, If you want to get rid of your teacher today, Just peel a banana, put it on the floor, And watch your teacher slide out the door.
Up the river, Down the lake, Teacher's got The stomach-ache.
Four more days and we are free From the school of misery. No more pencils, no more books, No more teacher's sassy looks.
Tonight, tonight, the pillow fight, Tomorrow's the end of school. Break the dishes, break the chairs, Trip the teacher on the stairs.

49

One for sorrow, two for joy,
Three for a kiss and four for a boy,
Five for silver, six for gold,
Seven for a secret never to be told.
Eight for a letter from over the sea,
Nine for a lover as true as can be.

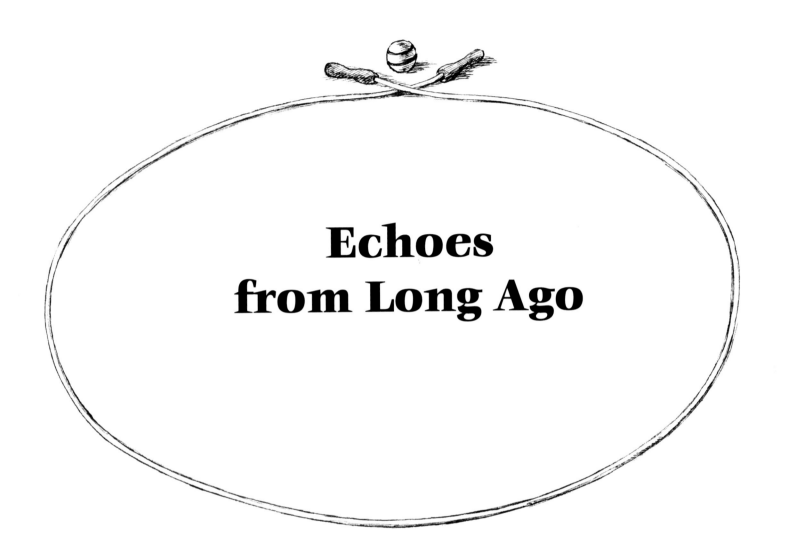

Echoes
from Long Ago

A woman to her son did utter,

Go, my son, and shut the shutter.

The shutter's shut,

the son did utter,

I cannot shut it any shutter.

There was a man called Michael Finigan,
He grew whiskers on his chinigin,
He shaved them off but they grew in ag'in,
Poor old Michael Finigan, begin ag'in.

The wind, the wind, the wind blows high,
The snow comes falling from the sky,
Mary Thomson says she'll die
If she doesn't get a fellow with a roving eye.

54

Round and round and round she goes,
And where she stops, nobody knows.
Point to the east, point to the west,
Point to the one that you love the best.

The doggie will not bite you, nor you, nor you... but you!

Queen Anne, Queen Anne sits in her sedan,
Fair as a lily, white as a swan,
A pair of white gloves are over her hands
And she is the fairest in all the land.
Buy my lilies, buy my roses,
Make them into pretty posies
For the maiden you will choose.

picked it up, And put it in his pocket, P-O-C-K-E-T, pocket.

As I went up  the ecky pecky road, I met a scabby donkey.

You one it, you two it,
You three it, you four it,
You five it, you six it,
You seven it, you ATE it!

Stockings red,
garters blue,
Trimmed all round
with silver,
A red, red rose
upon my head,
And a gold ring
on my finger.
Tell me, tell me,
where I was born,
Over the hills
among the green corn.
A B C D E F G H I J K ...

One, two, three, four,
Mary at the kitchen door.
Five, six, seven, eight,
Mary at the garden gate.

A
B
C
D
E
F
G
H
I
J   K
L
M
N
O
P   Q
R
S
T
u
W   V
X
Z Y

When Barney-boy was one, he learned to suck his thumb. Over Barney, over Barney, half past one. When Barney-boy was two, he learned to tie his shoe. Over Barney, over Barney, half past two. When Barney-boy was three, he always touched his knee. Over Barney, over Barney, half past three. When Barney-boy was four, he always touched the floor. Over Barney, over Barney, half past four. When Barney-boy was five, he learned to wink his eye. Over Barney, over Barney, half past five. When Barney-boy was six, he helped to pick up sticks. Over Barney, over Barney, half past six. When Barney-boy was seven, he watched the stars in heaven. Over Barney, over Barney, half past seven. When Barney-boy was eight, he always shut the gate. Over Barney, over Barney, half past eight. When Barney-boy was nine, he had a porcupine. Over Barney, over Barney, half past nine. When Barney-boy was ten, his pet it was a hen. Over Barney, over Barney, half past ten. When Barney-boy was eleven, he took a trip to Devon. Over Barney, over Barney, half past eleven. When Barney-boy was twelve, he learned to make a shelf. Over Barney, over Barney, half past twelve. When Barney-boy was grown, he sat upon a throne. Over Barney, over Barney, Barney-boy!

57

What's your name? Mary Jane. Where do you live? Down the lane. What do you keep?

On the mountain stands a lady,
Who she is I do not know.
All she wants is gold and silver,
All she wants is a nice young man.

Lady, lady, touch the ground,
Lady, lady, turn right round;
Lady, lady, show your shoe,
Lady, lady, run right through.

58

A little shop. What do you sell? Ginger pop. How many bottles do you sell in a day? Twenty-four. Now go away!

Water, water, wallflowers,
growing up so high,
We are all maidens
and we must all die,
Except for Nellie Ritchie,
the youngest of us all,
She can dance
and she can sing,
And she can do
the Highland Fling:
Fly, fly, fly for shame,
Turn your back
and look again!

Now you are married
we wish you joy,
First a girl
and then a boy,
Seven years after,
a son and a daughter,
Pray, young couple,
come kiss together,
Kiss her once,
kiss her twice,
Kiss her three times over.

SOAP

No more pencils, no more books,
No more teachers' ugly looks,
No more things that bring us sorrow
'Cos we won't be here tomorrow.

Down in the valley where
the green grass grows,
There stands Miss Hutchinson all on her own.
She grows, she grows, she grows so sweet,
The worst of it all,
she's got sweaty feet.

Pounds,
shillings,
pence,
Teacher has no sense.
She came to school
To act the fool,
Pounds,
shillings,
pence.

Davy, Davy, fie for shame,
Kissed the girls in a railway train.

Charlie, Charlie, chuck, chuck, chuck,
Went to bed with three young ducks.

Davy, Davy,
Stick him in the gravy.

Sweetly sings the donkey
As he goes to the grass,
He who sings so sweetly
Is sure to be an ass.

Bobby, Bobby, number nine,
Sewed his breeks with binder twine.

Made you look, made you cry,
Made you buy a penny pie.
Look up, Look down,
You're the biggest fool in town.

Adam and Eve and Pinch Me Tight
Went down to the sea to bathe.
Adam and Eve were drowned—
Which of the three was saved?

Georgie Porgie, pudding and pie,
Kissed the girls and made them cry,
When the boys came out to play,
Georgie Porgie ran away.

Dan, Dan, the dirty old man,
Washed his face in a frying pan.

Pinkety, pinkety,
Thumb to thumb,
Wish a wish and it's sure to come.
If yours comes true,
Mine will come true,
Pinkety, pinkety,
Thumb to thumb.

White horse,
white horse,
Bring me good luck.
Good luck to you,
Good luck to me,
Good luck to
everyone I see.

See a pin and pick it up,
All the day you'll have good luck.
See a pin and let it lay,
Bad luck you'll have all that day.

A dimple in your chin,
Your fortune will come in;
A dimple in your cheek,
Your fortune's far to seek.

MAGPIES

One for sorrow,
Two for mirth,
Three for a wedding,
Four for a birth.

Other Collections of Schoolyard Rhymes

Cole, Joanna, ed. *Anna Banana: 101 Jump-Rope Rhymes.* New York: Morrow Junior Books, 1989

Cole, Joanna, and Calmenson, Stephanie, eds. *Miss Mary Mack and Other Children's Street Rhymes.* New York: Morrow Junior Books, 1990

Delamar, Gloria T. *Children's Counting-Out Rhymes, Fingerplays, Jump-Rope and Bounce-Ball Chants and Other Rhythms.* Jefferson, NC: McFarland and Co., 1983

Fowke, Edith, ed. *Sally Go Round the Sun.* Toronto: McClelland & Stewart, 1969

Fraser, Amy Steward, ed. *Dae Ye Min' Langsyne? A Pot-pourri of Games, Rhymes and Ploys of Scottish Childhood.* London: Routledge & Kegan Paul, 1975

Gomme, Alice B. *The Traditional Games of England, Scotland, and Ireland.* 2 vols. New York: Dover, 1964

Greenaway, Kate. *Kate Greenaway's Book of Games.* New York: St. Martin's Press, 1987

Grugeon, Elizabeth. "Children's Oral Culture: A Transitional Experience." In *Oracy Matters: The Development of Talking and Listening in Education,* edited by Margaret MacLure, Terry Phillips and Andrew Wilkinson. Milton Keynes, England: Open University Press, 1988

Kane, Alice. *Songs and Sayings of an Ulster Childhood.* Toronto: McClelland & Stewart, 1983

Knapp, Herbert, and Knapp, Mary. *One Potato, Two Potato ... The Secret Education of American Children.* New York: W.W. Norton, 1976

Milnes, Gerald. *Granny, Will Your Dog Bite and Other Mountain Rhymes.* New York: Alfred A. Knopf, 1990

Opie, Iona and Peter. *Children's Games in Street and Playground.* New York: Oxford University Press, 1984

Opie, Iona and Peter, eds. *I Saw Esau: The Schoolchild's Pocket Book.* Cambridge, MA: Candlewick Press, 1992

Opie, Iona and Peter. *The Lore and Language of School Children.* London: Oxford University Press, 1989

Peer, Willie van. "Counting Out: Form and Function of Children's Counting-Out Rhymes." In *Oracy Matters: The Development of Talking and Listening in Education,* edited by Margaret MacLure, Terry Phillips and Andrew Wilkinson. Milton Keynes, England: Open University Press, 1988

Pierce, Maggi Kerr. *Keep the Kettle Boiling: Rhymes from a Belfast Childhood.* Belfast: Appletree Press, 1983

Rosen, Michael, and Steele, Susanna, eds. *Inky Pinky Ponky: Children's Playground Rhymes.* London: Collins Picture Lions, 1982

Skolnik, Peter L. *Jump Rope!* New York: Workman Publishing Co., 1974

Withers, Carl, ed. *I Saw a Rocket Walk a Mile.* New York: Holt Rinehart and Winston, 1965

Withers, Carl, ed. *A Rocket in My Pocket: The Rhymes and Chants of Young Americans.* New York: Henry Holt, 1948

Yolen, Jane, ed. *Street Rhymes Around the World.* Homesdale, PA: Wordsong, Boyd Mills Press, 1992

Zola, Meguido, ed. *By Hook or By Crook: My Autograph Book.* Montreal: Tundra Books, 1987

Index of First Lines

Index of Rhymes by Type

Book design and type by N.R. Jackson
Set in Veljovic type
Hand lettering done by the artist
Maryann Kovalski's illustrations are a combination of
historic nineteenth-century woodcuts and pen-and-ink drawings
on Arches medium tooth paper.

Film by Bergman Graphics Limited
Printed and bound in Hong Kong by
Wing King Tong Company Limited